Happy Habits: Fun Poems for Little Ones

This book belongs to:

_____

_____

_____

Contents

1. "Morning Munchies" (about breakfast)
2. "Wonderful Water" (about water)
3. "Fruit Fiesta" (about fruits)
4. "Veggie Rainbow" (about vegetables)
5. "Snack Time" (about snacks)
6. "Rainbow Plate" (rainbow on the plate)
7. "Sparkling Smiles" (brushing teeth)
8. "Splash and Wash" (washing up)
9. "Magic Comb" (combing hair)
10. "Soapy Adventures" (washing hands)
11. "Bubble Bonanza" (bath time)
12. "Dress for the Weather" (dressing according to the weather)
13. "Morning Moves" (exercise)
14. "Sporty Fun" (sports)
15. "Doctor's Visit" (visiting the doctor)
16. "Safe Steps" (road safety rules)
17. "Green World" (caring for nature)
18. "Every Drop Counts" (saving water)
19. "Animal Friends" (caring for animals)
20. "Learning Every Day" (learning every day)
21. "Book Time" (reading time)
22. "Helping Hands" (helping others)
23. "Learning to Forgive" (forgiving friends)
24. "Relax and Unwind" (rest time)
25. "Neat and Tidy" (keeping the room clean)
26. "Dreamy Night" (bedtime)

Morning Munchies

Every morning when you wake,
A healthy breakfast you should take!
Oatmeal, yogurt, eggs so bright,
Start your day just right!

Fruits and toast, some milk to drink,
Makes you strong, quicker than a wink!
Eat it up, enjoy the taste,
Healthy foods - no need to waste!

Wonderful Water

Water, water, cool and clear,
Drink it daily, far and near.
It keeps you fresh, it keeps you fine,
Fill your cup, oh, little mine!

In the morning, noon, and night,
Water's a delight just right.
Gulp it, sip it, take a swig,
Water's the dance, and you the jig!

Fruit Fiesta

Fruits are yummy, oh so sweet,
Apples, bananas, berries to eat.
Crunchy, munchy, juicy too,
Good for me and good for you!

Red strawberries, blue blueberries,
Yellow bananas fun like fairies.
Eat them whole or in a pie,
Reach up high towards the sky!

Veggie Rainbow

Green and red, yellow too,
Vegetables are good for you.
Crunchy carrots, spinach leaves,
Healthy eating, nature weaves.

Broccoli trees and tomato red,
Eat your veggies, go ahead!
Good for eyes, and skin, and hair,
Vegetables take you everywhere.

Snack Time

When you feel a little peckish,
Choose a snack that is delish.
Carrots, apples, nuts, and cheese,
Healthy snacks are sure to please.
Avoid the sweets and chips, oh my,
Choose snacks that make your health fly high!
Crunch and munch on snacks so great,
Healthy eating feels just right!

Rainbow Plate

Eat a rainbow every day,
Foods of colors, bright and day.
Red tomatoes, green peas,
Yellow peppers, eat with ease.

Every color has a place,
On your plate, a healthy base.
Different nutrients, different taste,
Eat with joy, no need for haste!

Sparkling Smiles

In the morning, bright and sunny,
Brush your teeth to make them funny.
Up and down, then side to side,
Clean them well, don't let them hide!

At night before you go to bed,
Brush them well, my sleepyhead.
Twinkle, twinkle, little star,
Clean and bright your teeth they are!

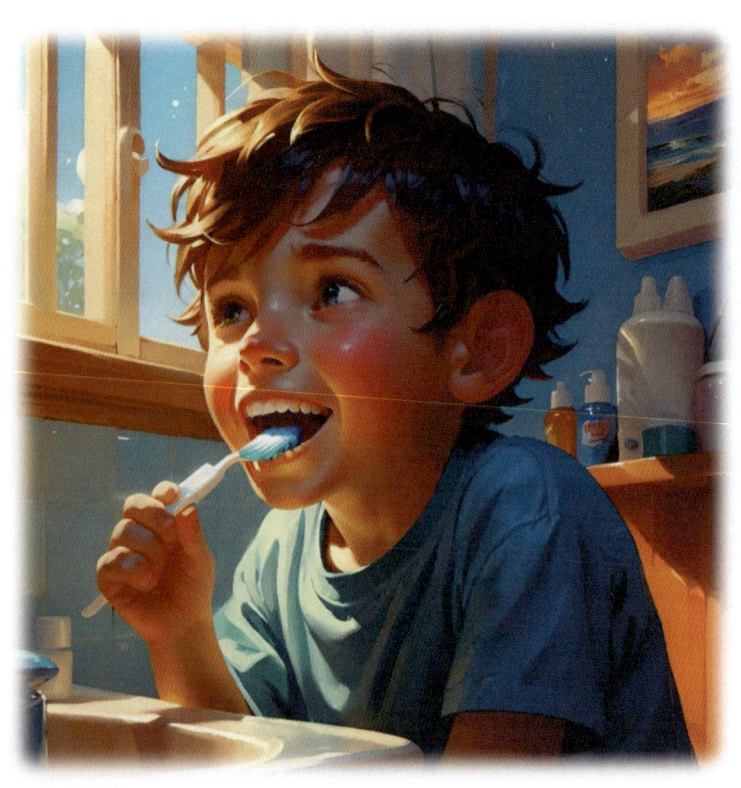

Splash and Wash

Splash some water on your face,
Wake up fresh, embrace the grace.
Soap it up, then wash it off,
Clean and bright, don't scoff!

Morning wash makes you glow,
Healthy skin, it's good to show.
Wash your face, start the day,
Happy, clean, and ready to play!

Magic Comb

Every morning, every night,
Brush your hair with all your might.
Gently, gently, stroke by stroke,
No more tangles, no more choke.

Long or short, curly or straight,
Make your hair look really great.
Brush it smooth, take your time,
Healthy hair feels so fine!

Soapy Adventures

Scrub, scrub, scrub your hands,
Wash them well, just as planned.
Before you eat, after play,
Keep the germs so far away!

Bubbles up, rinse them down,
Wash those germs right out of town.
Sing a song while you scrub,
Splash and laugh in the suds hub!

Bubble Bath

It's bath time now, don't you frown,
Let's wash off the dirt from playing in town.
Warm water ready, bubbles galore,
Jump in the tub, explore and soar!
Soap up your arms, and soap your knees,
Cleanse away germs with the greatest of ease.
Scrub scrub scrub from your toes to your chin,
Bath time fun, and you'll come out all grin.

Dress for the Weather

Sunny days or when it rains,
Dress right, to beat weather's games.
Sunny hat or rainy boots,
Weather's fun with all its routes!
When it's cold, wear your coat,
Warm and snug around your throat.
In the heat, wear something light,
Stay cool, from morning till night!

Morning Moves

Stretch up high to touch the sky,
Bend down low, let's not be shy.
Twist and turn, jump on your feet,
Morning exercise is sweet.
Start your day, the healthy way,
Energy for work and play.
Stretch and smile, reach the star,
Active kids will travel far!

Sporty Fun

Jump and run, play tag and hide,
Spin around, slide and glide!
Playing sports is so much fun,
Underneath the shining sun.

Ride a bike or jump in place,
Happy smile upon your face.
Healthy bodies, healthy minds,
In active play, joy you'll find!

Doctor's Visit

When you're sick or just for a check,
Visiting the doctor is always best.
They'll check your height and check your weight,
With a stethoscope, listen to your heart's rate.
A shot or a pill, maybe a bandage too,
Doctors know just what to do.
So brave and strong, you must be,
Doctors help keep us healthy!

Safe Steps

When you walk or ride your bike,
Safety first is what we like.
Helmets on when on a ride,
Safe and sound with every stride.

Look both ways when you cross the street,
Green light's go; red light's beat.
Hold hands tight when you walk,
Safety talks in every talk!

Green World

Trees and bushes, flowers, grass,
Walking slowly, not too fast.
Breathe the air, so fresh, so sweet,
Nature's bounty, can't be beat!

Caring for our world is key,
Plant a tree, or maybe three.
Recycle, reuse, reduce,
Loving Earth, no excuse!

Every Drop Counts

Water is precious, water is life,
Let's save it amid our strife.
Shorter showers, fixing leaks,
Every drop counts, week by week.

Turn off taps, don't let it run,
Saving water can be fun!
Use it wisely, spread the word,
Let every water-saving tip be heard!

Animal Friends

Animals big, animals small,
Let's take care of them all!
Pets at home or wild in the park,
They need love from light till dark.

Feed them right, keep them clean,
Treat all life as a royal queen.
Animals depend on our care,
Show them love, always be fair.

Learning Every Day

Every day's a chance to learn,
Open a book, take your turn.
Science, math, art, and more,
Knowledge opens every door.

Ask questions, be curious,
In learning, be furious!
Grow your mind, set it free,
Learn something new, happy you'll be!

Book Time

Open a book, take a look,
In your cozy, little nook.
Stories of lands far and near,
Read and learn, cheer and cheer.

Dragons, fairies, magic spells,
Exciting tales that the book tells.
Reading makes you smart and wise,
In every book, a new surprise!

Helping Hands

Helping out is always good,
Makes you feel just like you should.
Share your toys, lend a hand,
Together strong, together stand.

Friends are there through thick and thin,
With helping hands, we always win.
Share a smile, give a hug,
Kindness is a cozy rug.

Learning to Forgive

When friends make mistakes, as everyone will,
Learning to forgive is a valuable skill.
"Sorry" and "It's okay," simple to say,
Healing words that brighten the day.
Letting go of grudges, making amends,
Helps us stay happy, helps us stay friends.
Forgiveness is powerful, try and you'll see,
Makes your heart lighter, sets anger free!

Relax and Unwind

After play, it's time to rest,
Quiet time is sometimes best.
Read a book or sing a song,
Resting helps us grow strong.

Lie down soft, close your eyes,
Dream of clouds and butterfly skies.
Rest your body, rest your mind,
Peace and calm, you're sure to find.

Neat and Tidy

Keep your room so neat and clean,
Toys away, floors all sheen.
Put things back where they belong,
Clean and tidy, sing a song!

Books on shelves and clothes in drawers,
Vacuum carpets, mop the floors.
When your space is neat and tight,
Resting here feels just right!

Dreamy Night

When the moon begins to rise,
Close your eyes, close your eyes.
Sleeping helps you grow and rest,
Making tomorrow your very best.

Snuggle up in your cozy bed,
Pillow soft beneath your head.
Dream of places fun and new,
Sleep well, my dear, I love you.